Jesus Wakes the Little Girl

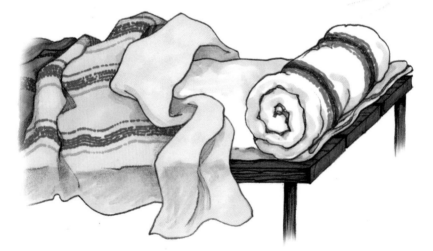

The story of Jairus's daughter

Matthew 9:18–19, 23–26; Mark 5:21–24, 35–43; and Luke 8:40–42, 49–56 for children

Written by Joanne Bader

Illustrated by Michelle Dorenkamp

CONCORDIA PUBLISHING HOUSE · SAINT LOUIS

One day when Jesus took a boat
To go across the sea,
A large crowd waited on the shore
In nearby Galilee.

They welcomed Him when He arrived.
They were expecting Him,
When suddenly a man appeared
Whose face looked very grim.

This man, who ruled the synagogue,
Had "Jairus" as his name.
He fell right down at Jesus' feet
To tell just why he came.

"My only daughter, twelve years old,
Is near to death," he said.
"Please come and lay Your hands on her
So she will live instead!"

Now Jesus went along with him
And the disciples too.
The whole crowd followed close behind
To see what He would do.

So Jairus led them to his house—
He was in a hurry.
He had great faith in Jesus' pow'r.
He tried not to worry.

Along the way there came a man
Who then to Jairus said,
"The Teacher is not needed, for
Your daughter now is dead!"

But Jesus overheard his words
And told the ruler then,
"You must not fear. Only believe—
She will be well again."

When they got to the ruler's house,
They could hear loud weeping.
But Jesus said, "She is not dead.
She is only sleeping."

The mourners there all laughed at Him,
For they knew she was dead.
They'd all been right inside the house—
Some very near her bed.

Then Jesus sent the crowd away,
And when they all were gone,
He took her mom and dad inside
With Peter, James, and John.

He held her hand and said to her,
"Now, little girl, arise!"
And she got up and walked around
Before their wondering eyes.

"Get her some food, for she must eat,"
That's just what Jesus said.
And all the people gathered there
Could see she was not dead.

Jesus is God! He raised the girl!
Her parents were amazed.
They knew it was a miracle.
They thanked Him and they praised.

Their little girl was well again.
She now had life and breath,
And she could run and talk and play.
Jesus had conquered death.

As Jesus rose from His own death,
We, too, will rise someday.
And we will go to heaven with Him
Who took our sins away.

Dear Parents,

This amazing story describes a wonderful miracle of healing. It gives us an example of the power of faith. Jairus, whose daughter was dying, went and pleaded with Jesus to come to his home. He trusted that if Jesus would just lay His hands on her, she would be well and live. How great was his faith!

The story illustrates the awesome power of God. The little girl was raised from the dead and healed from her illness as soon as Jesus took her hand and told her to arise. How great is the power of God!

This story also offers a special opportunity to talk about death with your child. Because of Jesus' death on the cross and His resurrection, He conquered death once and for all. So we need not fear death. We, too, will fall asleep and wake up to see His radiant face in eternity. To Him be the glory!

The Author